NATIVE AMERICANS

A VISUAL EXPLORATION

by S.N. PALEJA

introduction by KEVIN LORING

the
B!G
PICTURE

annick press
toronto + new york + vancouver

Book Design and Art Direction by Backyard Creative
Illustration by Dafne Sagastume
Edited by Paula Ayer
Proofread by Tanya Trafford

Annick Press Ltd.

We acknowledge the support of the Canada Council for the Arts, the Ontario Arts Council, and the Government of Canada through the Canada Book Fund (CBF) for our publishing activities.

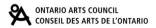

ONTARIO ARTS COUNCIL
CONSEIL DES ARTS DE L'ONTARIO

Cataloging in Publication
Paleja, S. N. (Shaker Natvar)
        Native Americans : a visual exploration / S.N. Paleja ; introduction by Kevin Loring.

(The big picture)
Includes bibliographical references and index.
Issued also in electronic format.
ISBN 978-1-55451-485-4 (bound).

        1. Indians of North America—Canada—Juvenile literature. 2. Indians of North America—Juvenile literature. I. Title. II. Series: Big picture (Annick Press)

E77.4.P34 2013   J970.004'97   C2012-906447-5

Published in the U.S.A. by
Annick Press (U.S.) Ltd.

Printed in China

Distributed in Canada by:
Firefly Books Ltd.
66 Leek Crescent
Richmond Hill, ON
L4B 1H1

Distributed in the U.S.A. by:
Firefly Books (U.S.) Inc.
P.O. Box 1338
Ellicott Station
Buffalo, NY 14205

Visit us at: www.annickpress.com

table of contents

Welcome

Native American people are as different as the land they come from. They can be found from the Arctic Circle to the deserts of the south, from the East Coast to the West Coast, and across all the land in between. Wherever they live, Native people have adapted and thrived for many generations. We are reminded of their long history in everything from the names of our cities, rivers, and mountains, to inventions like the toboggan and snowshoes. Today, Native Americans are one of the fastest-growing populations in the United States and Canada. With an increasing number of prominent artists and leaders, their influence and voices continue to grow.

The book you are holding is an exciting **snapshot** of the many races and cultures of the indigenous peoples of North America, from prehistoric times to today. With tools such as infographics, maps, and charts, *Native Americans: A Visual Exploration* builds understanding about the first peoples of this continent. For instance, the section on housing shows how ingenious Native people were in adapting to their unique environments—whether it was a temporary house made of blocks of ice in the Arctic, or a permanent adobe dwelling built into the side of a cliff in the Southwestern United States. You'll read about the variety of languages spoken by Native Americans, their vast trading networks, and the many uses of a bison. Some of the information in this book might surprise you—for certain you'll make many fascinating new discoveries.

Why do we use the term **"Native American"** throughout this book? The indigenous peoples of Canada and the United States

Making Contact

When did the first explorers arrive, and what was the effect on Native populations?

CHAPTER 5

Page 32

have hundreds of other names, but it's complicated to list them all. When we talk about Native Americans, we aren't referring to a single group of people, but to a whole continent of distinct peoples, organized by tribe or nation, each with their own culture, identity, language, and history.

The author has gathered information from a **variety of sources**—not just research material, but stories, myths, and legends that have been passed down through generations of indigenous people. Sometimes experts or local tribes disagree about what they think might have happened because there is no written record from long ago, but new information and discoveries are always surfacing that help provide a better understanding.

Throughout their history, many indigenous tribes throughout North America used pictographs—drawings on rock or cave walls—to tell their stories. These amazing ancient records were coded with symbols that had great meaning. This book echoes that **pictograph tradition** by using dynamic and colorful visual cues to tell the story to a new generation.

The topic of Native Americans is immense, but this book begins the exploration of an exceptional people through the "Big Picture" of who they were and how they lived. I hope it will inspire you to explore more deeply the rich and fascinating world of Native Americans.

Kevin Loring is a member of the Nlaka'Pamux First Nation.

Where did they come from?

The Native Americans were the first people to live in the Americas—many thousands of years before European explorers and settlers arrived. How did they discover a new land?

There's evidence humans first reached Siberia's eastern edge about 40,000 years ago. The land bridge probably started to emerge around the same time.

SIBERIA

During the ice age, Beringia was a mild, ice-free refuge, covered in plants and grass. Ice may have closed off passages to both Asia and North America, trapping people in Beringia for as long as 20,000 years—long enough to develop genetic differences from their Asian ancestors.

Bridging Two Continents

Look at a map of the Americas today. It's obvious the only way to get on or off the continent is by water or air. But thousands of years ago, humans were able to walk from Asia to North America over a "land bridge" connecting the continents. For this to happen, though, all the conditions had to be right.

Shoreline 20,000 years ago

PACIFIC OCEAN

Beringia

Often called a land bridge, Beringia was actually a huge mass of land connecting Asia's eastern edge with what's now Alaska. At its peak, it would have been 1,600 km (1,000 miles) across.

Ice Age

The coldest point of the last ice age was about 20,000 years ago. Because so much water was locked up in ice, ocean levels were much lower than they are today, exposing more land.

Today: 120 m (400 ft) deeper

20,000 years ago

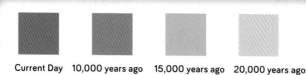

Current Day   10,000 years ago   15,000 years ago   20,000 years ago

The Youngest Continent

How long have modern humans been on each continent?

Africa
about 200,000 years

Asia
about 125,000 years

Australia
about 50,000 years

Europe
about 40,000 years

Americas
about 20,000 years

ARCTIC OCEAN

BERINGIA

The earliest migrants probably had no idea they had discovered a new continent. They were hunter-gatherers following their food sources as large animals moved east.

ALASKA

Shoreline today

All Native Americans are believed to be descended from the several thousand people who lived in Beringia.

N
W   E
S

Frozen Planet

How much of the Earth is covered in ice?

30%
20,000 years ago

10%
Today

Shallow Waters

The Arctic is by far the shallowest of the world's oceans, so when the climate cools and water levels drop, more land emerges.

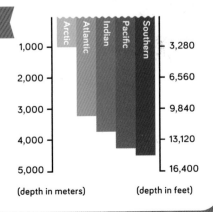

		Arctic	Atlantic	Indian	Pacific	Southern	
1,000							3,280
2,000							6,560
3,000							9,840
4,000							13,120
5,000							16,400

(depth in meters)   (depth in feet)

How did they get here?

At least 15,000 years ago and possibly much earlier, the first Native Americans migrated from Beringia into what's now North America. They may have traveled down the coast, taken an ice-free passage through the continent, or both. Discoveries by archaeologists, linguists, and genetic researchers are always revealing more about when and how the first people came to America.

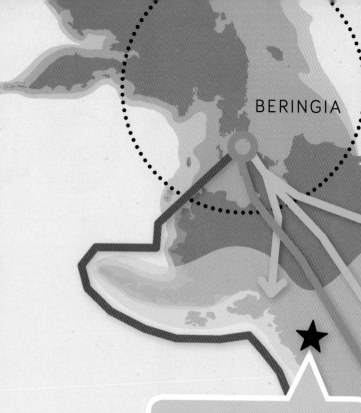

BERINGIA

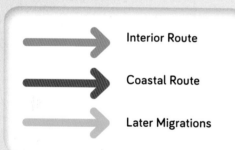

→ Interior Route

→ Coastal Route

→ Later Migrations

A Growing Culture

By about 10,000 years ago, the climate in North America had become more stable, and conditions were much like today's. Native Americans were able to migrate more widely and cultivate crops, and the population grew quickly. Many tribes today have their own stories, passed down through generations, describing how their people migrated thousands of years earlier.

Yukon, Canada
Mammoth bones that look like they were chipped by humans were found in a cave, dating back over 20,000 years.

The earliest arrivals in North America may have traveled down the West Coast, either by boat or on foot. Because most of the coastline at that time is now deeply submerged underwater, it's hard to find evidence of these coastal migrants.

Paisley Caves, Oregon
Fossilized human feces and hunting tools from at least 14,000 years ago were found here.

Monte Verde, Chile
Campsite remains show that humans lived at this site in South America over 14,000 years ago.

Around 11,000 years ago, smaller groups moved out of Beringia in at least two separate waves. These groups would become the speakers of Eskimo-Aleut and Na-Dene languages (including the Navajo and Apache).

NORTH AMERICA

Some migrants may have taken an ice-free route, through the continent, either before the worst of the ice age or as the glaciers receded.

Clovis, New Mexico

Once thought to be the first settlement in the Americas; Clovis people made distinctive tools from bone and ivory, dating from around 13,000 years ago.

Ice covered much of North America, as far south as what's now New York City, until about 13,000 years ago.

Meadowcroft, Pennsylvania

One of the oldest known human habitation sites in North America—at least 16,000 years old.

Native American Timeline

40,000–11,000 YA (years ago)

Waves of people cross the Bering Strait and settle throughout the Americas.

20,000 YA

Peak of the ice age.

1700s–1800s

Diseases and wars continue to kill many Native Americans, while laws are passed by state and federal governments to take away their rights and land.

1607

Jamestown is founded in Virginia by English colonists. Captain John Smith is captured by Native American Chief Powhatan and saved from death by the chief's daughter, Pocahontas.

Early 1600s

French explore and settle Mississippi River; many Southeast tribes fight with Europeans.

1570

Use of Native pottery declines as metal kettles become available by trading furs with Europeans.

European fur trade in Subarctic (and later on the Northwest Coast); beaver, mink, and otter hunted nearly to extinction.

1600s–1700s

1550

Horses are brought to the Southeast and the Plains. Wild horses quickly spread across the Plains, and are tamed and used by Native Americans.

1709

A slave market is erected at the foot of Wall Street in New York City. African-Americans and Native Americans are sold as property to the highest bidder.

1740s–1790s

Northeast tribes at war with Europeans; after their homes and crops are burned, many flee to Canada.

1870

Bison are nearly extinct, causing a crisis for Plains tribes who rely on them for survival.

1741

Russian traders arrive in Alaska. By mid-1800s, local Aleut population drops by 80 percent.

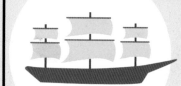

European and Asian traders arrive on Northwest Coast.

Late 1700s

1848

Natives massacred in California Gold Rush. By 1872, Native American population in California drops from 300,000 to 30,000.

13,000 YA
Clovis peoples in the Southwest make distinctive stone tools.

8,000 YA
Native Americans begin to domesticate plants, such as corn, squash, and sunflowers.

12,000–10,00 YA
Ice age ends; Bering land bridge closes. As the climate warms, people spread across the continent.

1492
Columbus's voyage marks the beginning of European exploration to the Americas.

3,000 YA
Agriculture is developed in many areas.

1000
Norse sailors establish settlements in what are now the Maritime Provinces of Canada.

300
The bow and arrow is invented on the Plains.

★ **Beginning of Common Era (CE)**

1200
First large winter villages built on the Northwest Coast. A large hunting and slave trading network flourishes until the late 1700s.

Pueblo and cliff dweller cultures emerge in the Southwest, while in the Southeast, mound builders create large planned towns.

700–1300

1871
US government passes Indian Appropriation Act, which takes away tribes' rights to form treaties with the government.

1885
Cree, Ojibwe, and Métis rebel against Canadian government.

1924
Native Americans get the right to vote in the US. However, they do not have full voting rights in all states until 1962.

1960
Native Americans get the right to vote in Canada.

The Apache, the last tribe to actively wage war with the US government, surrender.

1880s

1890
Hundreds of unarmed Sioux are massacred for practicing their Ghost Dance religion.

Many Native American tribes win the right to govern themselves; large sections of land are returned.

1930s–1990s

How did they live?

As the climate warmed, Native Americans established more permanent communities and cultures that flourished for thousands of years. Where their ancestors were nomads, following the few animals and plants they relied on for food, later Native Americans began to cultivate crops, live in larger groups that were settled at least part of the year, and develop complex and varied societies that grew out of their relationships to the land.

Regions

Anthropologists often study Native Americans by **culture areas,** or geographic regions where tribes have common traits. Within each of these areas there can be a huge diversity of cultures, languages, and customs.

LEGEND

warm/hot	rain	flat
temperate	snow	mountains
cool/cold	varied	rolling hills
dry/desert		boreal forest
		varied (plateaus basins, gorges)

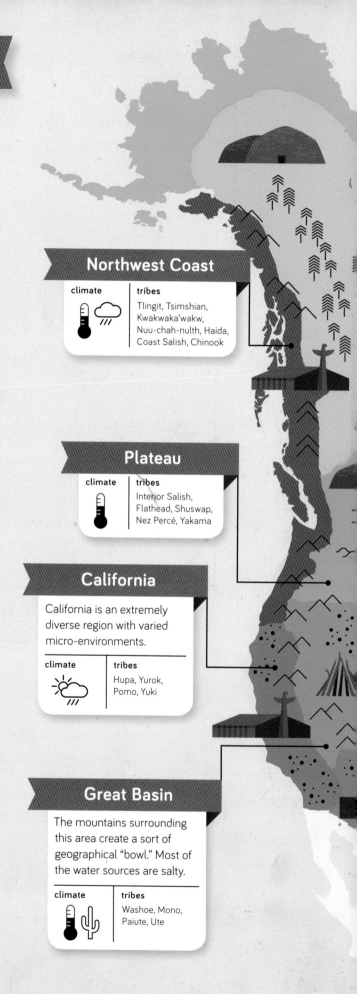

Northwest Coast

climate	tribes
	Tlingit, Tsimshian, Kwakwaka'wakw, Nuu-chah-nulth, Haida, Coast Salish, Chinook

Plateau

climate	tribes
	Interior Salish, Flathead, Shuswap, Nez Percé, Yakama

California

California is an extremely diverse region with varied micro-environments.

climate	tribes
	Hupa, Yurok, Pomo, Yuki

Great Basin

The mountains surrounding this area create a sort of geographical "bowl." Most of the water sources are salty.

climate	tribes
	Washoe, Mono, Paiute, Ute

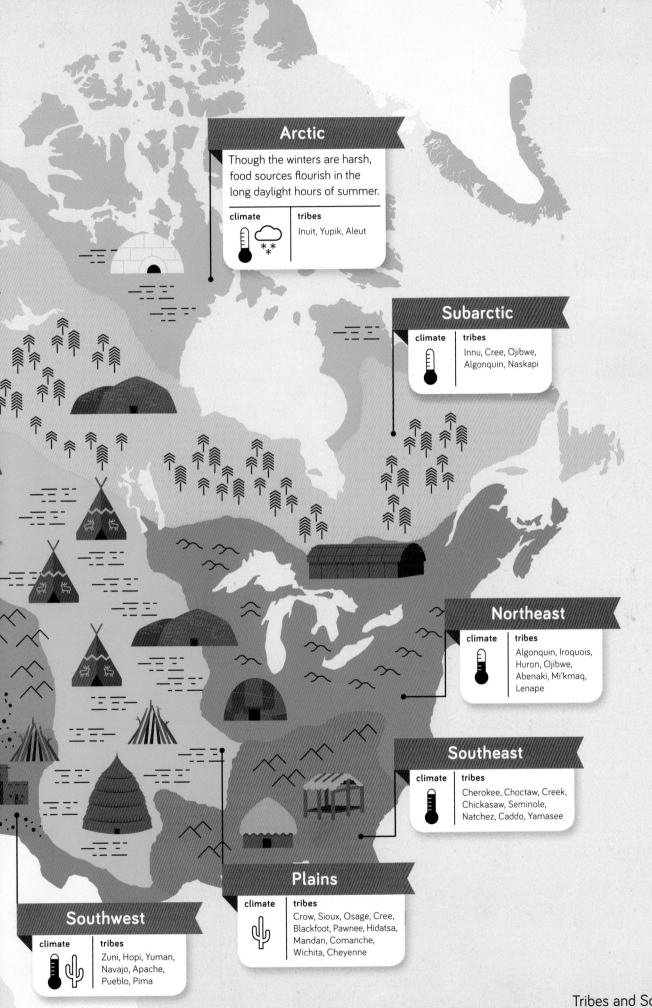

Arctic

Though the winters are harsh, food sources flourish in the long daylight hours of summer.

climate	tribes
	Inuit, Yupik, Aleut

Subarctic

climate	tribes
	Innu, Cree, Ojibwe, Algonquin, Naskapi

Northeast

climate	tribes
	Algonquin, Iroquois, Huron, Ojibwe, Abenaki, Mi'kmaq, Lenape

Southeast

climate	tribes
	Cherokee, Choctaw, Creek, Chickasaw, Seminole, Natchez, Caddo, Yamasee

Plains

climate	tribes
	Crow, Sioux, Osage, Cree, Blackfoot, Pawnee, Hidatsa, Mandan, Comanche, Wichita, Cheyenne

Southwest

climate	tribes
	Zuni, Hopi, Yuman, Navajo, Apache, Pueblo, Pima

Where did they live?

A Native American living in the Arctic requires a different type of shelter from one living in the desert, or the rainforest. Tribes in different areas have vastly different materials available. If your tribe had to pick up and leave quickly to follow food sources, you'd also need a different type of housing from a tribe that stayed in the same place year-round.

Tepee

Tepees, often elaborately decorated with paintings of animals and hunting, needed to be set up and taken down quickly, a job that fell to the women.

occupants	materials	mobility
1		

Chickee

Chickees have a raised platform to keep snakes, crocodiles, and other swamp animals out of the house. But there are no walls, so during rainstorms, animal hides were attached to the frame as tarps. The palm plants used for thatching the roof are naturally waterproof and fire-repellent.

occupants	materials	mobility
1		

Brush Shelter

Small and quick to build, these temporary shelters are just for sleeping. They aren't tall enough to stand in. Many tribes used these for short times when out hunting in the wilderness, but tribes in warm, dry climates, such as the Apache, used them regularly.

occupants	materials	mobility
1-2		

Igloo

Though temperatures in the Arctic can be as cold as −45°C (−49°F), the temperature inside an igloo can reach up to 16°C (61°F). Not all Inuit people used igloos—some built sod houses, using a frame of whale bones.

occupants	materials	mobility
1-20		

LEGEND

 person

 family

 animal skin	snow	ice
bark	earth	mud
branches	wood poles	grass/straw
cane	wood	palm leaves
clay	leaves	sand

 permanent

mobile

 semi-permanent or seasonal

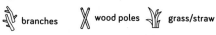

Earth House

Like a basement apartment, earth houses are built partly underground. Different varieties include Arctic sod houses, pit houses of the West Coast and Plateau, and Navajo hogans—the doors of which always face east.

occupants	materials	mobility
1-20		

Connect the colors to the map on pages 12-13 to see where these houses were built.

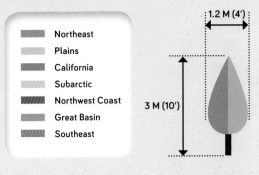

Northeast	
Plains	
California	
Subarctic	
Northwest Coast	
Great Basin	
Southeast	

1.2 M (4')
3 M (10')

Wattle & Daub

These houses take a lot of work to build, so they're good for people who stay in one place. They can last for up to 40 years and date back over 6,000 years. But don't try building one in a cold climate—you need warmth to dry the mud or clay that holds them together.

occupants	materials	mobility
1		

Wigwam

Because of the wigwam's round shape, rainwater runs off quickly and snow collects around it, providing insulation.

occupants	materials	mobility
1+		

Plank House

Built by coastal tribes who could fish year-round from a permanent base, plank houses have been used for at least 4,000 years.

occupants	materials	mobility
10-12		

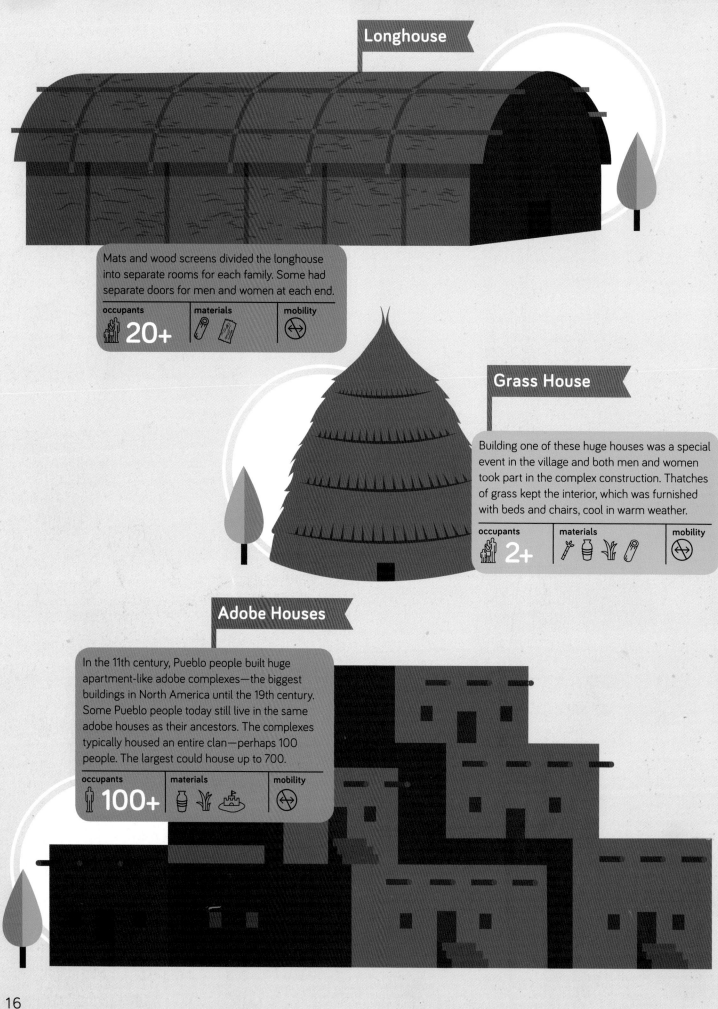

Longhouse

Mats and wood screens divided the longhouse into separate rooms for each family. Some had separate doors for men and women at each end.

occupants	materials	mobility
20+		

Grass House

Building one of these huge houses was a special event in the village and both men and women took part in the complex construction. Thatches of grass kept the interior, which was furnished with beds and chairs, cool in warm weather.

occupants	materials	mobility
2+		

Adobe Houses

In the 11th century, Pueblo people built huge apartment-like adobe complexes—the biggest buildings in North America until the 19th century. Some Pueblo people today still live in the same adobe houses as their ancestors. The complexes typically housed an entire clan—perhaps 100 people. The largest could house up to 700.

occupants	materials	mobility
100+		

What was life like?

Native American communities ranged from small groups of a few families to huge, complex cities. The largest was Cahokia, in what's now southern Illinois—the largest city in North America until the 18th century.

An Impressive City

People first lived in Cahokia around 700 CE. By 1100 it was the hub of an ancient culture that constructed mounds of earth and grew crops on a large scale. Building the city would have taken skilled planners and a huge workforce.

Population

Cahokia
1250 CE
20,000

London
1250
15,000

New York
1750
13,000

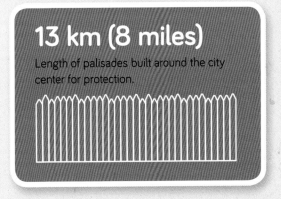

13 km (8 miles)

Length of palisades built around the city center for protection.

623,000 m³
(22 million cubic feet)

Amount of earth moved by workers to build Monks Mound, the focal point of the city and largest man-made earth structure in North America.

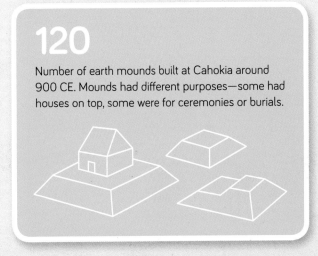

120

Number of earth mounds built at Cahokia around 900 CE. Mounds had different purposes—some had houses on top, some were for ceremonies or burials.

Typical Communities

Where food was scarce, the main social unit was small, mobile bands of people who were usually related. These groups might come together to form larger bands at certain times of the year. Where food was plentiful, tribes tended to establish larger, more permanent villages and towns.

| small bands | larger bands | independent tribelets* | villages | towns |

*A tribe could be divided into several independent groups, called tribelets.

Social Structures

While some tribes were egalitarian, with everyone in the tribe having a say in decisions, others were stratified, or divided, into higher and lower classes. Some even kept slaves—usually war captives from other tribes. Cultures where food was plentiful tended to have more rigid social divisions.

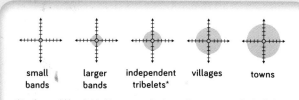

| less stratified | somewhat stratified | very stratified |

Kinship

Some Native American tribes were matrilineal, which means children and property belonged to the mother's clan, or family. Others were patrilineal, belonging to the father's clan, and some were bilineal—belonging to both sides.

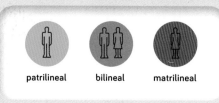

| patrilineal | bilineal | matrilineal |

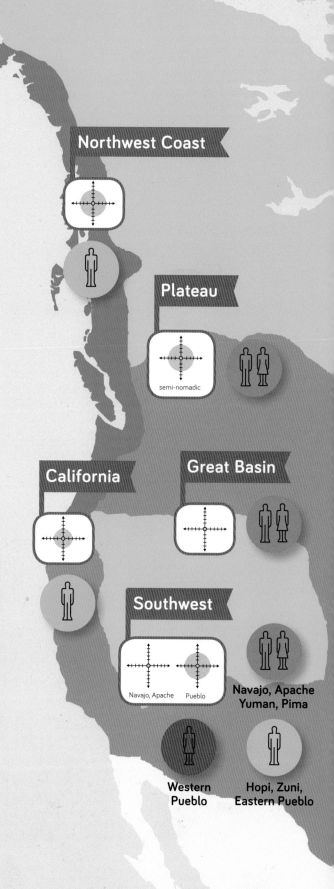

Northwest Coast

Plateau

semi-nomadic

California

Great Basin

Southwest

Navajo, Apache | Pueblo

Navajo, Apache
Yuman, Pima

Western
Pueblo

Hopi, Zuni,
Eastern Pueblo

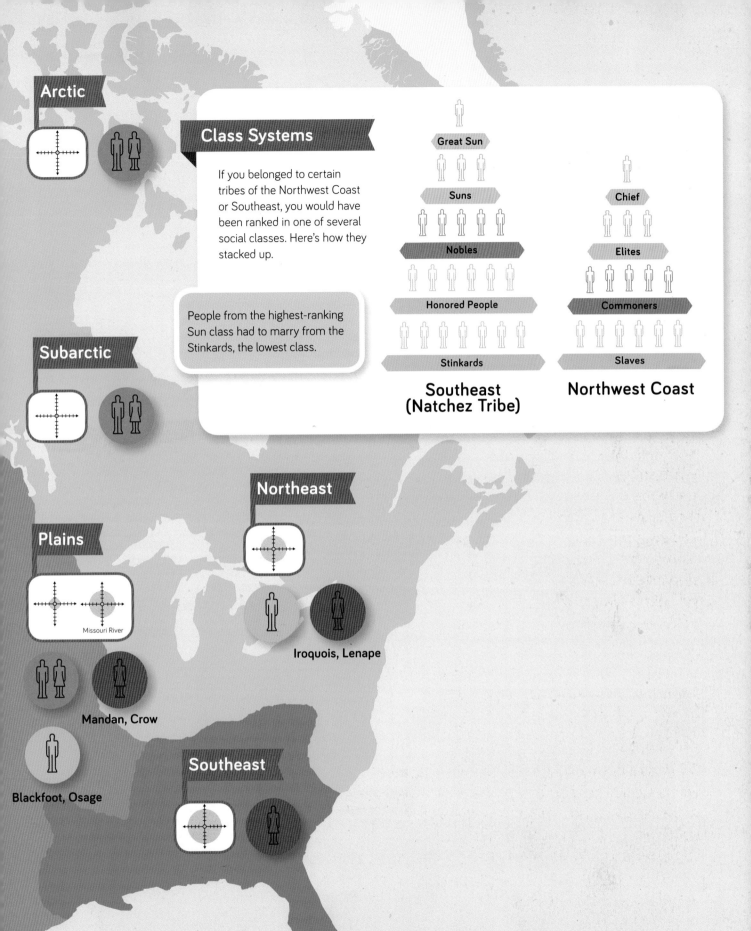

Arctic

Class Systems

If you belonged to certain tribes of the Northwest Coast or Southeast, you would have been ranked in one of several social classes. Here's how they stacked up.

People from the highest-ranking Sun class had to marry from the Stinkards, the lowest class.

Southeast (Natchez Tribe)
- Great Sun
- Suns
- Nobles
- Honored People
- Stinkards

Northwest Coast
- Chief
- Elites
- Commoners
- Slaves

Subarctic

Northeast

Iroquois, Lenape

Plains

Missouri River

Mandan, Crow

Blackfoot, Osage

Southeast

How did they eat?

Native Americans obtained their food from plants and animals in different ways, requiring a variety of tools and techniques. Some tribes relied on **hunting,** following herds of bison or caribou and developing sophisticated systems for killing them in large numbers. For coastal tribes, **fishing** was hugely important. In the South and Northeast, **farming** was well developed and Native communities used modern methods such as irrigation and crop rotation. **Gathering** of wild berries, acorns, and other foods also provided a major source of nutrients.

Farming

The Hopi, Navajo, and Cherokee tribes of the South were expert farmers, and usually harvested enough to dry and store for the winter. Northeastern tribes such as the Lenape and Iroquois planted crops but couldn't produce enough to last the year, so switched to hunting and gathering in winter.

plants	tools & techniques
corn, beans, squash, sunflowers, fruit and nut trees, cotton, tobacco	fire, irrigation, crop rotation, terracing, windbreaks, drying in sun

Fishing

The Inuit tribes of the North and the Tlingit and Coast Salish of the Northwest relied mostly on fishing for survival. Tribes caught fish and hunted marine mammals from canoes, or else set fish nets and wooden traps.

animals	tools & techniques
salmon, other fish, whales	bows and arrows, spears, harpoons, fish hooks, blowguns, wooden traps, lures, nets

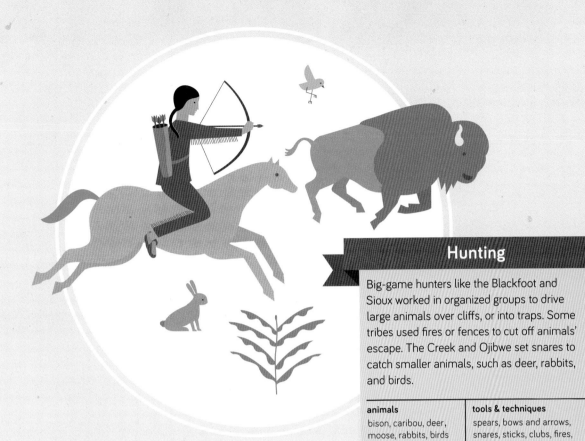

Hunting

Big-game hunters like the Blackfoot and Sioux worked in organized groups to drive large animals over cliffs, or into traps. Some tribes used fires or fences to cut off animals' escape. The Creek and Ojibwe set snares to catch smaller animals, such as deer, rabbits, and birds.

animals	tools & techniques
bison, caribou, deer, moose, rabbits, birds	spears, bows and arrows, snares, sticks, clubs, fires, fences, mass kills

Gathering

Gathering wild foods could be as simple as picking berries from a bush, or it could require special tools and knowledge, like tapping trees for maple syrup, or grinding acorns to produce edible flour. Women and children of a tribe were often responsible for the task of gathering.

plants & animals	tools & techniques
berries, acorns, nuts, roots, wild rice, maple syrup, insects, shellfish	hands, stone tools, mortars and pestles, drying in sun

What can you make with a bison?

The bison was a sacred and important animal for Plains Native Americans, who relied on it for nearly all their needs. The bison has been called a "walking department store" because it was a one-stop source for food, clothing, shelter, tools, weapons, and more.

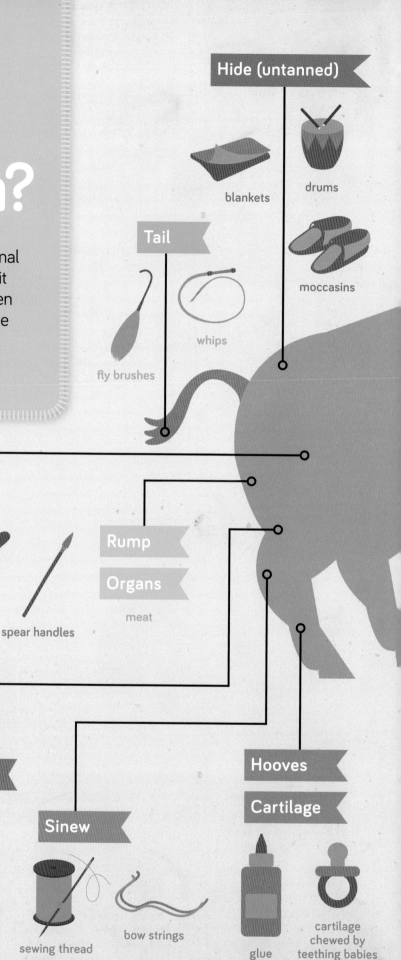

Hide (untanned)

blankets

drums

moccasins

Tail

whips

fly brushes

Bones

arrowheads

shovel

scrapers

knives

spear handles

Rump

Organs

meat

The tongue, liver, and other organ meats, which are high in vitamins and minerals, were considered the best meat. When there were plenty of bison, people would eat only these parts and feed the rest to dogs. Nowadays, it's the other way around—cheaper organ meats are ground into dog food, while people eat the more expensive cuts with fewer nutrients.

Blood

paint

Sinew

sewing thread

bow strings

Hooves

Cartilage

glue

cartilage chewed by teething babies

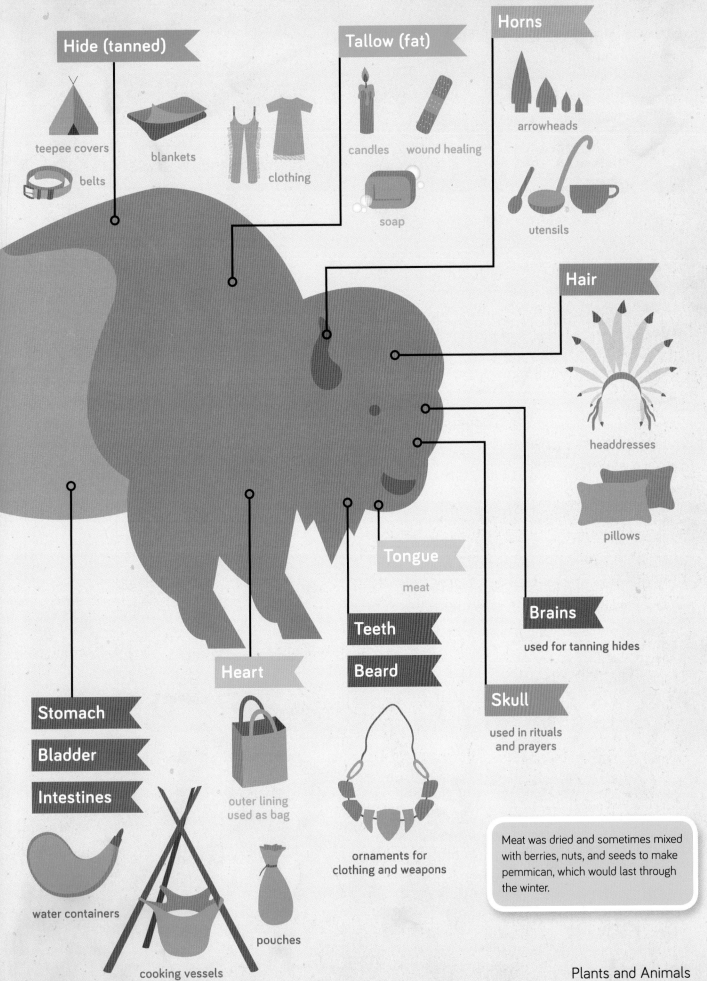

Hide (tanned)

teepee covers

blankets

belts

clothing

Tallow (fat)

candles

wound healing

soap

Horns

arrowheads

utensils

Hair

headdresses

pillows

Tongue

meat

Teeth

Beard

Heart

Brains

used for tanning hides

Skull

used in rituals and prayers

Stomach

Bladder

Intestines

water containers

cooking vessels

pouches

outer lining used as bag

ornaments for clothing and weapons

Meat was dried and sometimes mixed with berries, nuts, and seeds to make pemmican, which would last through the winter.

Man vs. Nature— who wins?

The landscape and wildlife of North America were transformed by developing Native American societies—and then again by the arrival of Europeans.

Shaping the Land

Over thousands of years, as the Native American population increased and their societies developed, they left their mark on the wilderness. They used fire to tame forests, planted orchards of fruit and nut trees, and created vast agricultural plantations.

Demand for Resources

Larger towns and settlements required a lot of resources. Around the largest city, Cahokia (page 17), animals were hunted to the point of scarcity, so many trees were cut down that the soil eroded away, and the site was eventually abandoned. Here's what a village of around 1,500 needed to survive.

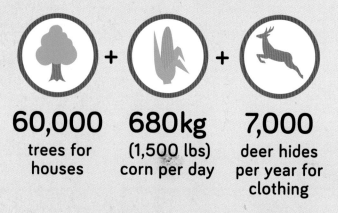

60,000
trees for houses

+

680kg
(1,500 lbs) corn per day

+

7,000
deer hides per year for clothing

Land Use

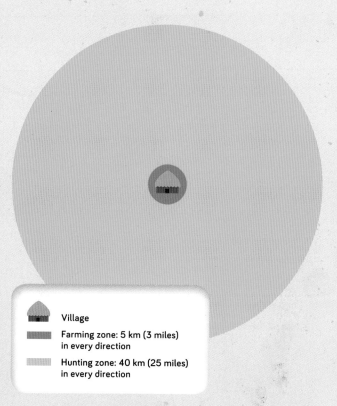

- Village
- Farming zone: 5 km (3 miles) in every direction
- Hunting zone: 40 km (25 miles) in every direction

Moving Faster

The introduction of horses to North America starting in the 1500s brought huge changes for Native Americans. Horses made it easier to travel quickly, trade and share knowledge with tribes farther away, and hunt more efficiently.

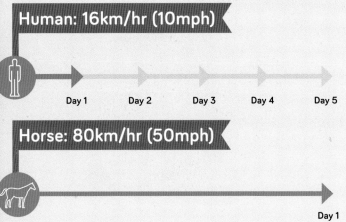

Human: 16km/hr (10mph)

Day 1   Day 2   Day 3   Day 4   Day 5

Horse: 80km/hr (50mph)

Day 1

Vanished Species

The earliest North Americans shared the land with many large mammals, including mammoths, sabertooth cats, beavers as big as bears, and giant armadillos that could roll into a ball as tall as a person. Climate change and hunting caused many to go extinct.

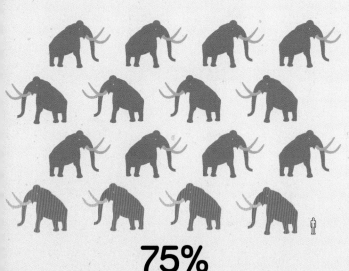

75%
disappeared 12,700 years ago

Disappearing Wildlife

Europeans killed bison in huge numbers for their skins. Combined with hunting by Native Americans, accelerated by the introduction of horses and guns, this nearly wiped the bison out altogether. Beavers almost disappeared as well because of the European quest for their pelts, used to make hats.

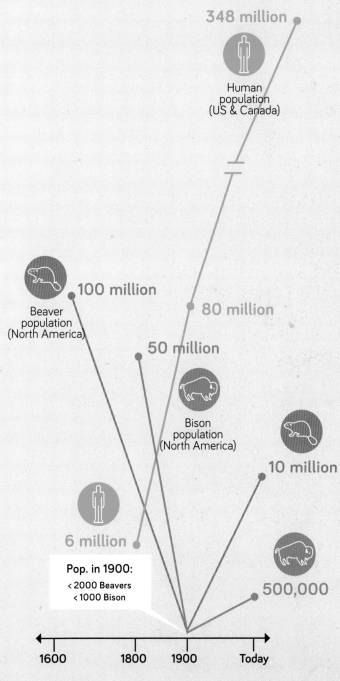

348 million

Human population (US & Canada)

100 million

Beaver population (North America)

80 million

50 million

Bison population (North America)

10 million

6 million

Pop. in 1900:
< 2000 Beavers
< 1000 Bison

500,000

1600   1800   1900   Today

What do they speak?

The indigenous languages of North America are incredibly diverse: there are more languages spoken by Native Americans in California alone than in all of Europe. However, many languages have disappeared since European contact, and many others have only a few remaining elderly speakers. Still, certain languages, such as Navajo, Ojibwe, and Cherokee, are thriving, and many tribes today are reclaiming and promoting the use of their mother tongues.

Language Families

Languages that have a common ancestor and share certain traits are classified into "families." (For instance, French, Spanish, and Italian are all part of the same family.) Some Native American language families include dozens of languages, while others have only a few.

57 Number of Native American language families*

2 Number of European language families*

*Pre-contact

Top Languages Today*

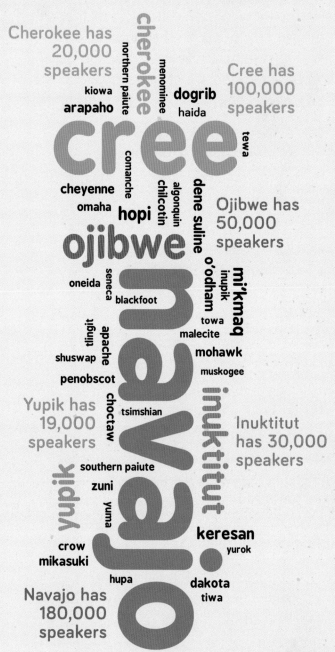

Cherokee has 20,000 speakers

Cree has 100,000 speakers

Ojibwe has 50,000 speakers

Yupik has 19,000 speakers

Inuktitut has 30,000 speakers

Navajo has 180,000 speakers

cherokee · northern paiute · menominee · kiowa · dogrib · arapaho · haida · cree · tewa · comanche · algonquin · chilcotin · dene suline · cheyenne · omaha · hopi · ojibwe · o'odham · inupik · mi'kmaq · oneida · seneca · blackfoot · towa · malecite · tlingit · apache · mohawk · shuswap · muskogee · penobscot · choctaw · navajo · inuktitut · tsimshian · southern paiute · zuni · yuma · keresan · crow · yurok · mikasuki · hupa · dakota · tiwa · yupik

*Approximate number of speakers, 2012

The Navajo language was in decline until World War II, when the US military used Navajo "Code Talkers" to transmit secret messages (Other languages, including Cree, Choctaw, and Cherokee, were also used). This led to a revival and today Navajo is the most spoken Native American language north of Mexico.

Place Names

Many place names in North America come from Native American tribe names or words. This map shows the state and province names with Native American origins (in yellow) and what they're thought to mean.

Some experts who study languages have found a link between certain Native American languages and languages spoken in Siberia, where their distant ancestors came from.

Native Americans had a spoken tradition, but no writing system, so there is little evidence of many languages that have been lost.

In some regions, tribes that spoke different languages communicated using a shared sign language.

Alaska "place the sea crashes against"

Yukon "great river"

Nunavut "our land"

CANADA "village"

Manitoba "the strait of the spirit"

Saskatchewan "swift flowing river"

Ontario "beautiful lake"

Quebec "strait"

Oregon "beautiful river"

Minnesota "cloudy water"

South/North Dakota "the allies"

Wisconsin "grassy place"

Michigan "great lake"

Massachusetts "by the range of hills"

Wyoming "by the big flat river"

Iowa "sleepy ones"

Ohio "it is beautiful"

Connecticut "long river"

Nebraska "flat river"

Illinois "best people"

Utah "the people"

Kansas "south"

Missouri "big canoe people"

Kentucky "meadow land"

Arizona "little spring"

Oklahoma "red people"

Arkansas "southern people"

Tennessee "a town"

Alabama "campsite"

Texas "friend"

Mississippi "great river"

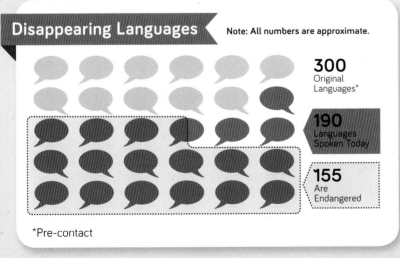

Disappearing Languages

Note: All numbers are approximate.

300 Original Languages*

190 Languages Spoken Today

155 Are Endangered

*Pre-contact

Pictographs

Some tribes used symbols called pictographs, which were written on rocks, cave walls, or pieces of bison hide. They were used to communicate, send warnings, or tell stories about hunting, battles, and daily life.

What do they believe?

Native American spirituality is rooted in the land, and focuses on sacred places and objects. In this view, human beings, animals, and even rocks, trees, and mountains hold spiritual power. Without a bible or holy book, tribes passed down spiritual stories—which often feature supernatural beings, spirits, and animals—through generations.

Life Rituals

Tribes had many types of ceremonies, often related to hunting, farming, changing seasons, and life passages. Many ancient ceremonies and traditions were lost after Europeans arrived, but others are still practiced today.

 Plains tribes perform the **sun dance** to reenact the creation of the world. Its purpose is to give thanks to the Creator, to pray for the renewal of the people and earth, and to make friendships with other groups.

 Native Americans in many regions used **sweat lodges,** similar to saunas, for purification and healing rituals. A frame of branches is covered with skins or a blanket, with a pit in the center filled with hot rocks. To create steam, water is thrown on the rocks. Sweat lodges were banned in many places by the US and Canadian governments. However, today they are still used by many tribes.

 Generosity is an important aspect of Native American spirituality. Northwest Coast peoples hold **potlatches**—ceremonial gatherings where tribes distribute property and gifts.

Birth
In some tribes, pregnant women had to give birth in a special lodge. Babies were often named according to special customs or for the last relative who had died.

Boy Childhood
Boys often accompanied their fathers on hunting and fishing trips, and might hunt by themselves for birds and small game. Accomplishments, like killing their first deer, were celebrated.

Girl Childhood
Girls helped their mothers with gathering and planting, food preparation, sewing, and household tasks. They were rewarded for achievements like making their first basket.

Male Puberty
In many tribes, at 14 or 15, a boy would be sent into the wilderness for a vision quest. He spent several days alone fasting and might be visited by an animal spirit or take a plant that made him hallucinate. He would come back on his way to becoming a man, with the vision to guide him for the rest of his life.

Female Puberty
In many tribes, when a girl had her first period, she would be sent away from the tribe for a few days to a few months. She was considered very powerful at this time and had to follow rules about food, clothing, and grooming. The tribe would mourn the girl who had left, and hold a feast to welcome the woman who came back.

Marriage
Marriage practices varied. Some tribes were monogamous; in some, a husband had more than one wife; and in a few, a wife sometimes had more than one husband. If your wife (or husband) died, you would probably marry her sister (or his brother).

Death
Native Americans had no common beliefs about an afterlife. Some believed humans were reincarnated as another person, or an animal. Some believed humans returned as ghosts, or went to another world. Others thought it was impossible to know what happened after death. Some tribes destroyed the house where a death took place.

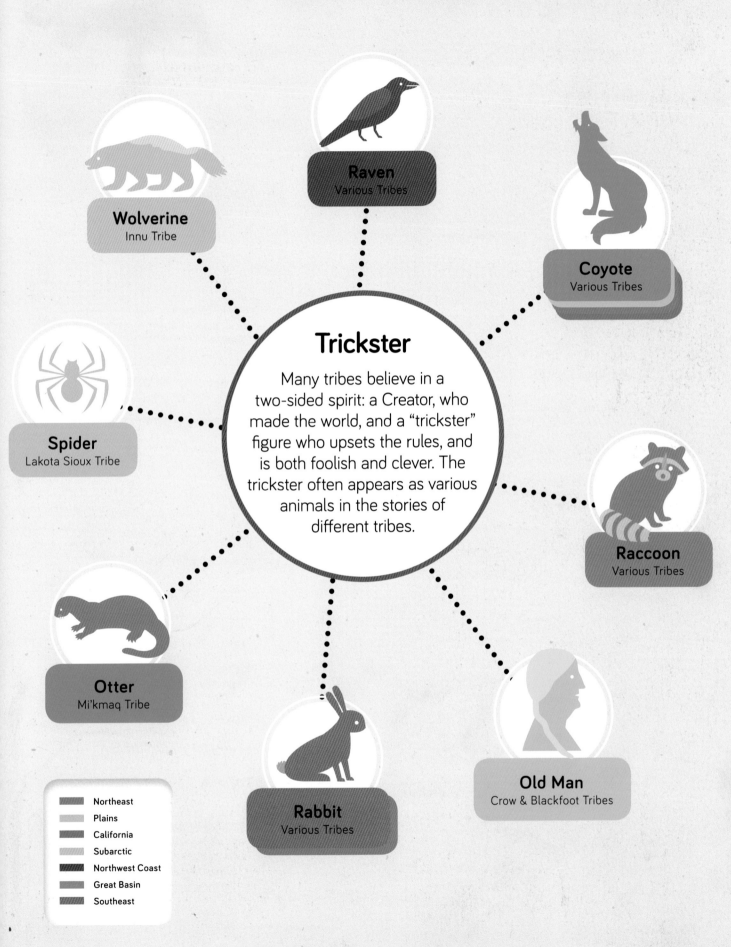

Raven
Various Tribes

Wolverine
Innu Tribe

Coyote
Various Tribes

Trickster

Many tribes believe in a
two-sided spirit: a Creator, who
made the world, and a "trickster"
figure who upsets the rules, and
is both foolish and clever. The
trickster often appears as various
animals in the stories of
different tribes.

Spider
Lakota Sioux Tribe

Raccoon
Various Tribes

Otter
Mi'kmaq Tribe

Rabbit
Various Tribes

Old Man
Crow & Blackfoot Tribes

Northeast
Plains
California
Subarctic
Northwest Coast
Great Basin
Southeast

What do they make?

Native Americans are responsible for many inventions and innovations that we still use today, from snowshoes to sunscreen. Each region is also known for particular styles of clothing, arts, crafts, and technology.

Sports and Games

Plains: hacky sack

Northeast: ice hockey, lacrosse

Southeast: hoop and pole game

Various: field hockey

Hockey

A version of hockey was played by Native Americans, on ground or ice, by both men and women.

Arts & Crafts

Plains: large drums, pottery, feathered headdresses

Southwest: baskets, pottery, blankets and rugs, sand paintings, masks

Great Basin: baskets, rock art

Southeast: baskets, pottery, ceremonial objects

Northeast: dreamcatchers, porcupine quill boxes, tobacco pipes

Northwest Coast: totem poles, carvings, wooden masks

California: baskets, pottery, rock art

Insect repellent

The Coast Salish rubbed wild onion on their skin to repel bugs; Northeastern people applied bear fat, while the Cherokee mixed bear fat with ground goldenseal plant roots.

Transportation

Plains: travois, small boats made of saplings and bison skin

Northwest Coast: large boats, dugout canoes

Subarctic: snowshoes, toboggans

Arctic: snowshoes, dogsleds

Northeast: birchbark canoes

Clothing

Plains: leather clothing

California: feathered clothing

Subarctic: fur clothing

Arctic: fur clothing, mukluks

Various: moccasins

Medicine & Healing

Southeast: insect repellent

Northeast: diapers (from absorbent sphagnum moss), insect repellent

Northwest Coast: herbal remedies, insect repellent

Various: herbal remedies, sunscreen, tooth cleaner (from a plant root)

Moccasins

Just about every tribe in every region wore a type of moccasin, or soft leather shoe. You could tell which tribe someone belonged to by the distinctive style, beadwork, or painted designs.

Travois

The travois was a Plains technology consisting of two poles in the shape of a V, with a platform across for carrying loads. Dogs would pull the narrow end of the V, while the open end dragged on the ground.

Food

Plains: smoked meat

Arctic: pemmican

Northeast: maple syrup, smoked fish

Southeast: succotash (stewed corn and beans)

Sunscreen

Some modern sunscreens still contain sunflower seed oil, or ingredients from wallflower or agave plants, first used as sun protection by Native Americans.

Tools

Subarctic: spear-throwers

Northeast: wooden tools

Northwest Coast: fishing tools and nets, duck decoys

California: obsidian tools

Whose land is it?

There's no firm evidence Native Americans had any contact with outsiders until about 1000 CE, meaning the continent was probably isolated for thousands of years. After the arrival of European explorers, starting in 1492, Native American populations and societies were transformed, to devastating effect. Over the next few hundred years, all of the Americas came under the control of Europeans.

1000 CE: Norse

500 years before Columbus, Norse sailors (sometimes called Vikings) sail across the Atlantic and establish the first known European settlement in L'Anse aux Meadows, Newfoundland. They fish, and probably trade with indigenous tribes. By 1013, possibly because of conflict with Native Americans, they leave the continent.

LEGEND

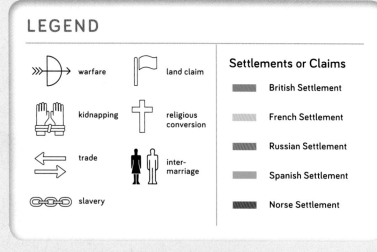

»»—⟩	warfare
🧤	kidnapping
⇄	trade
⛓	slavery
⚑	land claim
✝	religious conversion
👥	inter-marriage

Settlements or Claims

- British Settlement
- French Settlement
- Russian Settlement
- Spanish Settlement
- Norse Settlement

1492: Spanish

Christopher Columbus, looking for a sea route to Asia, instead reaches an island in the Bahamas. Over four voyages he explores the Caribbean and Central and South America, bringing home gold and spices. Many indigenous people in these lands are enslaved, executed, or taken captive to be shown in Europe as curiosities. Though Columbus never sets foot in North America, word of the "New World" spreads rapidly to Europe, and other countries rush to explore and colonize it.

1497: British

John Cabot reaches what's probably Newfoundland and claims it for the King of England. He's thought to be the first European since the Norse to set foot on North American land, though he believes he's reached the northeast coast of Asia. Soon after, Europeans establish fishing bases in the region, trading iron and household goods to Native Americans in exchange for furs. By 1578 there are 350 European fishing vessels in Newfoundland waters.

1513: Spanish

Vasco Núñez de Balboa crosses Panama and becomes the first European to reach the Pacific coast. He immediately claims the entire west coast of the continent for Spain. However, the Spanish don't actually colonize north of Mexico until 250 years later, when they settle northern California.

1529: Spanish

Hernando de Soto is the first European to explore deeper into the United States, from Florida to Arkansas. His expedition faces many battles with tribes, some of them extremely skilled, well-armed warriors. Some tribe members are captured and forced into slavery, or taken to slave markets in the Caribbean.

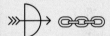

1513: Spanish

Juan Ponce de León claims Florida. There are battles with Native American tribes in which people are killed on both sides, and some tribe members are taken captive.

1524: French

Giovanni da Verrazano explores the Atlantic coast of North America, from Florida to Newfoundland, and claims it for France. He's the first European to see much of the east coast of the US, including what's now New York. He's also the first to provide written descriptions of the Native Americans along the coast. He kidnaps a Native American child to take back to Europe, as proof that he reached the New World.

1534: French

Jacques Cartier explores the Gulf of St. Lawrence region in eastern Canada. He's first welcomed by the Iroquois people, but they turn against him when he claims their territory and erects a large cross. Cartier kidnaps two Iroquois and takes them to France, bringing them back to Canada to serve as guides. Later he seizes about 10 more Iroquois; all but one die in France.

1607: British

Jamestown in Virginia is established as the first permanent English settlement. The Powhatan tribe are at first friendly and provide the settlers with food and help, but English thievery turns the tribe against them. In 1622 the Powhatan attack the colony, killing nearly a third of the settlers.

1715-16: British

An alliance of Yamasee, Creek, and other tribes fight English expansion into their territory.

1598: Spanish

Spanish settle in the Southwest, and battle with the Pueblo peoples. Missionaries intent on converting the region's inhabitants to Catholicism torture and execute Native Americans who refuse to abandon their traditional spiritual practices. Many continue to practice their religion in secret.

1610: British

Henry Hudson explores the Hudson Bay region, searching for a "Northwest Passage" to Asia. The fur trade begins in the north. In 1670, the Hudson's Bay Company is granted control over the entire north of Canada for the next two centuries. The company builds trading relationships with the Cree, Innu, and Inuit peoples.

1732: Russian

Russians begin establishing colonies in Alaska, and down the Northwest Coast as far as California, to hunt for furs. They treat the Native peoples as servants, holding villages hostage, stealing food, abusing Natives, and forcing them into labor. The well-armed Tlingit tribe on the Northwest Coast fight them off and profit by charging tolls for passage through waterways. By the early 1800s, intermarriage between Russian men and Native women improves relations.

1738: French

French traders initiate contact with the tribes of the northern Plains. The Mandan tribe gains a reputation as especially good negotiators. By the end of the 18th century, many European traders are living among Plains tribes. The arrival of horses and guns also transforms the region.

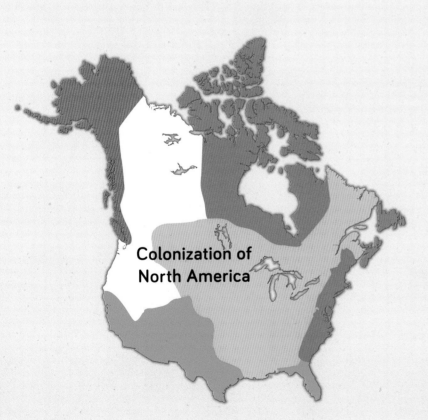

Colonization of North America

- France
- Great Britain
- Spain
- Russia
- No European claim

1750

By the mid 1700s, most of the continent has been claimed or settled by European powers. For the next century, they continue to expand into new territory, and fight and negotiate with local tribes and each other for possession of land.

What did they trade?

Trade was one of the biggest drivers of exploration, as Europeans sought valuable furs from wild animals to sell back home. In exchange, the new products they provided to Native Americans—metal tools, pots and pans, knives, guns, and much more—transformed their everyday lives.

What Did Native Americans Trade for Pelts?

9% blankets, kettles, pots & pans

23% beads, buttons, cloth, combs, mirrors, stockings

44% fish hooks, guns, axes, gunpowder, knives

24% tobacco & alcohol

Which Skins Did Europeans Want?

Eastern North America

bear   deer   skunk

Northern Canada (Arctic/Subarctic)

beaver   ermine

Plains

bison

Northwest Coast

sea otter

 =

11 beaver pelts   1 gun

 **=**

8 beaver pelts   1 gallon of rum

 **=**

6 beaver pelts   1 large kettle

  =

1 beaver pelt   2 combs

100,000 beaver pelts

were exported per year (at peak) to Europe for hats

Beaver hats became an expensive status symbol for Europeans, nearly causing the beaver's extinction in North America (page 25). By the mid-1800s, the fashion had shifted to silk hats—good news for the beavers.

Who Came Out Ahead?

European traders made huge profits off their exchanges with Native Americans, though Native Americans also benefited from new labor-saving tools and goods.

1 beaver pelt = 1 metal ax head

In Europe

1 beaver pelt = 20 metal ax heads

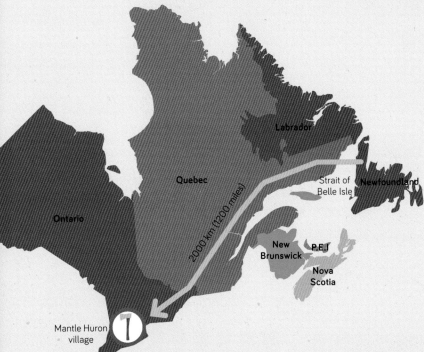

Labrador

Quebec

Strait of Belle Isle

Newfoundland

Ontario

2000 km (1200 miles)

New Brunswick

P.E.I.

Nova Scotia

Mantle Huron village

How Did Trade Spread?

Europeans' goods sometimes traveled into the continent faster than they did. A metal ax head discovered at the site of a Huron village in southern Ontario predated the arrival of Europeans in that area by about 100 years. The ax head was probably traded all the way from a whaling station in Newfoundland.

Forging Alliances

The fur trade was also a way to maintain good relations between different cultures. Fur traders, who usually went to North America as young, single men, often lived with or married high-ranking Native American women. The lower-class trappers had relationships with lower-ranking women. Their mixed-race children became a distinct cultural group known as the Métis.

How did so many die?

Nobody really knows how many Native Americans lived in North America before Columbus arrived; estimates range anywhere from 2 to 18 million. What is known for sure is that the population suffered a huge drop in the 150 years after Columbus, mostly due to the introduction of new diseases.

Germs Are Faster than People

By the time European settlers arrived, starting around 1600, Native Americans living in the eastern United States had already died off in huge numbers from new diseases, introduced to them decades before by explorers and sailors. The land the first Europeans saw was already far less populated than it had been a century earlier.

Spread of Diseases

New Diseases

Because Europeans lived in close contact with chickens, cows, pigs, sheep, and goats, they built up some resistance to the many diseases that originated in these animals. Native Americans rarely lived with animals, apart from dogs, so they had no immunity. When they were introduced to the Europeans' diseases for the first time, the effects were devastating.

How Many Died?

Even the Black Death in medieval Europe wasn't nearly as deadly as the epidemics that hit Native Americans.

cholera measles smallpox influenza bubonic plague malaria diptheria yellow fever typhus pertussis mumps

Death rates from diseases

Native Americans after European contact:

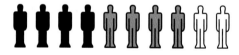

It's estimated 4 to 8 in 10 died between 1492 and 1700

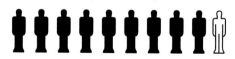

In some regions, it's known that 9 in 10 died

Deaths from the Black Death (plague):

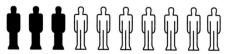

3 in 10 between 1340 and 1400

Violence

Disease was not the only cause of population loss. Many Native Americans died in warfare and conflict with European powers, settlers, and later the US government.

302
Number of years between the first Native American war with settlers (1622) and the end of the last armed conflict with the US government (1924).

40
Estimated number of wars between the US government and Native American tribes from 1775 to 1924.

30,000
Estimated number of Native Americans who died in these wars. It's likely many more deaths were not recorded.

Gold Rush

During the Gold Rush in California, the state paid settlers to quell Native "hostilities." Many peaceful tribal settlements were raided, just so settlers could claim a reward. About 4,500 Native Americans were violently killed, in addition to the many more who died of diseases brought by miners.

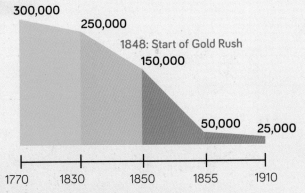

300,000
250,000
1848: Start of Gold Rush
150,000
50,000
25,000

1770   1830   1850   1855   1910

Native American population in California

Population Shifts

As the numbers of Native Americans dropped sharply due to diseases and violence, a mass influx of European settlers arrived. In the 19th century alone, 50 million immigrants came from Europe to North America.

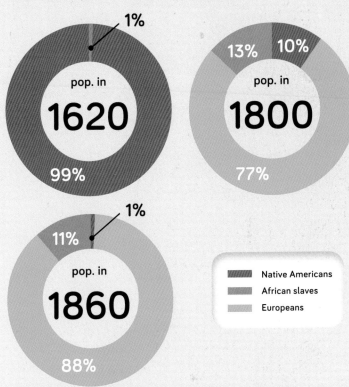

1%
pop. in
1620
99%

13% 10%
pop. in
1800
77%

1%
11%
pop. in
1860
88%

/// Native Americans
     African slaves
     Europeans

Forced Removal

The Indian Removal Act of 1830 allowed the US president to negotiate the removal of tribes from east of the Mississippi River, to free up land for white settlers. Many tribes defended their homelands through wars, courts, and negotiation. However, over the next decade, almost the entire Native population of the eastern US was forced by the government to move west. Many died from starvation and illness on the long, harsh journey, called the "Trail of Tears."

100,000
forced to move west

15,000
died*

*estimate

Who are they today?

Modern Native Americans are a diverse and growing group, represented by hundreds of tribes in every part of the US and Canada. Some still live on the lands of their ancestors, while others live in towns or cities. Here's a snapshot of Native Americans today.

Reservation or City?

Starting in the 1800s, most Native Americans in the US and Canada were forced to surrender their territory and given parcels of land called reservations (or reserves in Canada). During and after World War II, many left the reservations to enlist or find work. Today Native Americans are a more urban population, with more than half living outside reservations.

Percentage of Native Americans living in urban areas vs. reservations:

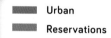

Urban
Reservations

55% 45%

65% 35%

Canada   **US**

Modern Tribes

There are 565 recognized tribal groups in the US and 615 in Canada. At least nine of these tribes have over 100,000 members.

Largest Tribes*

Cherokee: 819,105

Navajo: 332,129

Cree: 200,000

Ojibwe: 200,00

Choctaw: 195,764

Mexican Native American: 175,494

Sioux: 170,110

Apache: 111,810

Blackfoot: 105,304

*2010

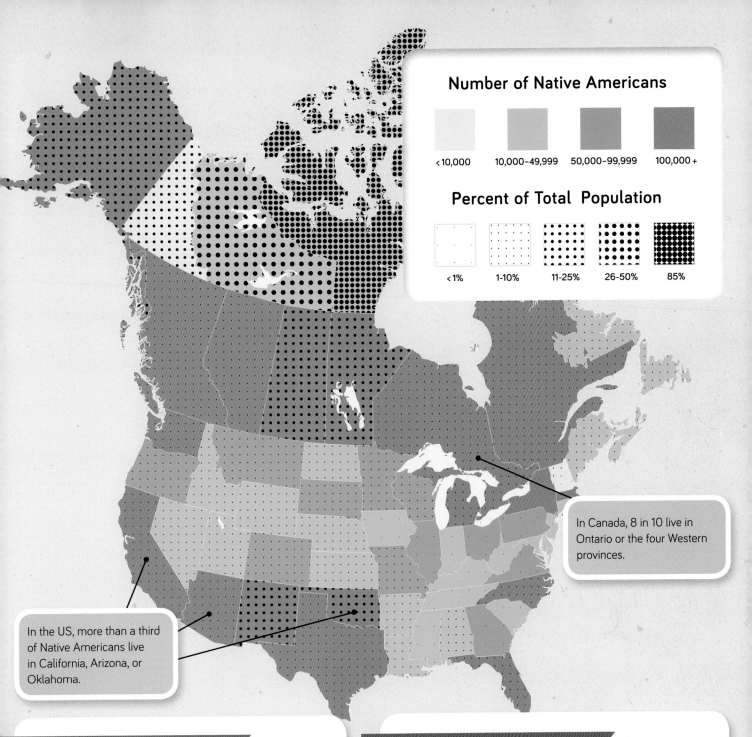

Number of Native Americans

| < 10,000 | 10,000–49,999 | 50,000–99,999 | 100,000 + |

Percent of Total Population

| < 1% | 1-10% | 11-25% | 26-50% | 85% |

In Canada, 8 in 10 live in Ontario or the four Western provinces.

In the US, more than a third of Native Americans live in California, Arizona, or Oklahoma.

Native Americans in Canada

3.8% of Total Canadian Population*

1.17 Million

60% First Nations
(698,025 people)

33% Métis
(389,785 people)

4% Inuit
(50,480 people)

3% combination or not identified

*2006 census

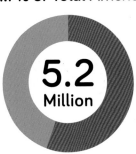

Native Americans in the US

1.7% of Total American Population*

5.2 Million

56% Native American alone
(2.9 million people)

44% Native American combined with other races
(2.3 million people)

*2010 census

Youth Revolution

The Native American population is a young one, and is increasing in nearly every state and province.

Median age* (US)

29
Native Americans

37
General Population

Median age* (Canada)

27
Native Americans

40
General Population

*Age at which half the population is younger, and half is older

A Growing Population

Growth between 2000-2010 (US)

27%
Native Americans

10%
General Population

Growth between 1996-2006 (Canada)

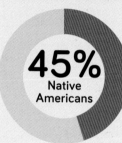

45%
Native Americans

8%
General Population

Military Service

Native Americans in the US and Canada have an admirable history of fighting to defend their countries. Even in World War I, when they were exempt from service, Natives volunteered in impressive numbers. During World War II, if the entire population had enlisted at the same rate as Native Americans, the draft wouldn't have been needed. Native women also served as nurses and helped the military effort.
By proportion, Native Americans contributed more than any other group towards winning the war.

64,000
Estimated number of Native Americans who served in the World Wars (Canada and US)

150,000
Native American Veterans of the US Armed Forces today

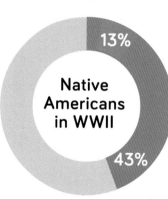

Native Americans in WWII

13%

43%

Native Americans who served in the war
(about 44,500 of 350,000)

Native Americans who contributed to the war effort
(about 150,000 of 350,000)

Number who received a medal of honor in WWII:

1 of every 35,000 American soldiers

1 of every 4,000 Native American soldiers

What issues do they face?

In Canada and the US, years of government policies displaced and isolated Native Americans and suppressed their languages and cultures. That history has contributed to inequality and social problems in some Native American communities.

What Were Boarding or Residential Schools?

Starting in the late 1800s, governments and churches established the system of boarding schools (called residential schools in Canada). Children as young as four were taken from their families, forced to cut their hair and wear uniforms, and punished for speaking their languages or displaying their cultures. The schools were breeding grounds for diseases like tuberculosis, which killed many. Some children were malnourished, or virtually enslaved. The legacy of these schools has left a profound effect on Native communities to this day.

150,000 children
Went to residential schools in Canada from 1879-1996

100,000 children
Went to boarding schools in the US from 1879-1996

Education Today

Many Native-run schools are working successfully to reverse the effects of boarding schools. But schools on reservations often receive less funding and have poor conditions, contributing to lower graduation rates.

Graduates from high school (US)

86% General Population   77% Native Americans

Graduates from high school (Canada)*

87% General Population   60% Native Americans

Poverty

Native Americans have about twice the poverty rate of the general population.

Living Below the Poverty Level 2010 (US)

 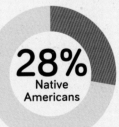

15% General Population   28% Native Americans

Living Below the Poverty Level 2006 (Canada)

 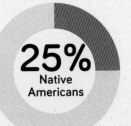

12% General Population   25% Native Americans

How do they make an impact?

Native Americans have always shown an amazing ability to adapt. Whether by choice or necessity, they have learned to live in new places and adopt unfamiliar ways of life, while staying rooted in their cultures. Today, Native Americans are leaders, innovators, and creators, with one foot in the modern world, and the other planted in that of their ancestors, honoring their traditions and values.

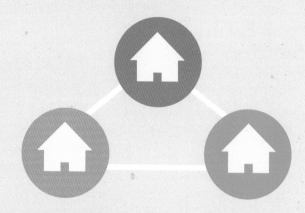

Leadership

Native Americans are active in politics at every level from local to international, and in a variety of organizations working for positive change and global peace. Many Native Americans in positions of power draw inspiration from traditional attitudes to leadership, rooted in responsibility, and believe that change is effected not by one person but through linked communities.

Environment

Native tribes and groups all across North America are working to respond to environmental challenges, whether it's protecting threatened plants or animals central to their lifestyles, or opposing pollution and damaging resource extraction on their land. Many tribes are also leading the way in adopting renewable forms of energy, such as wind and solar power.

Arts

Native Americans have achieved success in every artistic field, including visual arts, performing, music, and writing. Many Native artists today combine the cultural forms and stories of their tribes with modern techniques and ideas. For instance, the Canadian artist Brian Jungen, from the Dunne-za tribe, creates traditional-looking Northwest Coast aboriginal masks made out of Nike sneakers.

Technology

For Native Americans living in tribal communities, it is often much more difficult or expensive to access computers, telephones, and the internet. However, when Native Americans do have access to the internet, they use it at a higher rate than the national average—for blogging, social networking, sharing their own videos and music, and much more. Many tribes use websites as online repositories for promoting their languages, and preserving their stories and memories. They use the internet to build connections with others, discover and exchange information about their history, and talk about issues that might not get covered in the media.

Business

Modern Native Americans own businesses ranging from small family grocery stores to hugely profitable companies, in fields including tourism, agriculture, and entertainment. These business leaders often combine modern practices and innovations with the traditional values of their tribes.

Increase in Business Ownership[*]

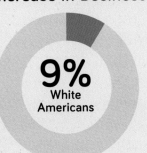 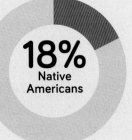

9% White Americans

18% Native Americans

*2002–2007

Percentage of Americans who have high-speed internet access at home[*]

72% of white Americans

50% of African-Americans and Hispanics

10% of Native Americans on tribal lands

*2011

Going Online

In some regions and among certain groups (like teens), internet use is high[*]

87%

of Native American teens in the Pacific Northwest have a social media profile

73%

use the internet every day

*2009

Selected Bibliography

Bradshaw Foundation with Stephen Oppenheimer. "Journey of Mankind." Bradshaw Foundation website. Retrieved April 20, 2012, from www.bradshawfoundation.com/journey

Cahokia Mounds State Historic Site. "Cahokia Mounds Timeline." Retrieved May 16, 2012, from www.cahokiamounds.org/explore/timeline

Curry, Andrew. "Ancient Migration: Coming to America." *Nature 485*, May 2, 2012. Retrieved July 15, 2012, from www.nature.com/news/ancient-migration-coming-to-america-1.10562

Dickason, Olive, and David T. McNab. *Canada's First Nations*. Don Mills, Ontario: Oxford University Press, 4th edition, 2009.

Encyclopaedia Britannica Online, s.v. "Native American." Retrieved August 30, 2012, from www.britannica.com/EBchecked/topic/1357826/Native-American

Giese, Paula. "Native Pre-Contact Housing." Retrieved May 9, 2012, from www.kstrom.net/isk/maps/houses/housingmap.html

Gray, Linda. *First Nations 101*. Vancouver: Adaawx Publishing, 2011.

Hey, Jody. "On the number of New World founders: A population genetic portrait of the peopling of the Americas." *PLoS Biology,* June 2005, 3(6): e193.

Kehoe, Alice B. *North American Indians.* Toronto: Pearson, 3rd edition, 2005.

Lassieur, Allison. *Before the Storm: American Indians Before the Europeans.* Markham, Ontario: Fitzhenry & Whiteside, 2002.

Lewis, Orrin, Laura Redish, and Nancy Sherman. Native Languages of the Americas website. Retrieved June 11, 2012, from www.native-languages.org

Morgan, Thomas D. "Native Americans in World War II." Excerpted from *Army History: The Professional Bulletin of Army History,* No. 35 (Fall 1995). Retrieved October 17, 2012, from www.shsu.edu/~his_ncp/NAWWII.html

Moseley, Christopher (ed.). *Atlas of the World's Languages in Danger.* Paris: UNESCO Publishing, 3rd edition, 2010. Retrieved July 16, 2012, from www.unesco.org/culture/en/endangeredlanguages/atlas

Norris, Tina, Paula L. Vines, and Elizabeth M. Hoeffel. "The American Indian and Alaska Native Population: 2010." U.S. Census Bureau. Retrieved September 21, 2012, from www.census.gov/prod/cen2010/briefs/c2010br-10.pdf

Podruchny, Carolyn, and Laura Peers (eds.). *Gathering Places: Aboriginal and Fur Trade Histories.* Vancouver: UBC Press, 2010.

Ray, Arthur J. *An Illustrated History of Canada's Native People.* Toronto: Key Porter, 2010.

Reich, David, et al. "Reconstructing Native American Population History." *Nature 488,* August 16, 2012. Retrieved August 31, 2012, from www.nature.com/nature/journal/v488/n7411/full/nature11258.html

Silvey, Diane. *The Kids Book of Aboriginal Peoples in Canada.* Toronto: Kids Can Press, 2005.

Statistics Canada. "Aboriginal Statistics at a Glance." Retrieved September 20, 2012, from www.statcan.gc.ca/pub/89-645-x/89-645-x2010001-eng.htm

Selected Bibliography (continued)

U.S. Census Bureau. "American Indians By the Numbers." Retrieved September 30, 2012, from www.infoplease.com/spot/aihmcensus1.html#ixzz29gvhFixH

Veterans Affairs Canada. "Aboriginal-Canadian Veterans." Retrieved October 17, 2012, from www.veterans.gc.ca/eng/history/aboriginal

Further Reading

Encyclopædia Britannica. *Native Peoples of the Americas.* Chicago: Encyclopædia Britannica, 2010.

Ipellie, Alootook, with David MacDonald. *The Inuit Thought of It.* Toronto: Annick Press, 2007.

Landon, Rocky, with David MacDonald. *A Native American Thought of It.* Toronto: Annick Press, 2008.

Mann, Charles C. *Before Columbus.* New York: Atheneum Books for Young Readers, 2009.

Waldman, Carl. *Atlas of the North American Indian.* New York: Facts on File, 3rd edition, 2009.

Index

S.N. Paleja has appeared as an actor in film, television, and theater across Canada. His fiction has been published in *The Dalhousie Review,* and he is currently working on his first novel. He lives in Vancouver, British Columbia.

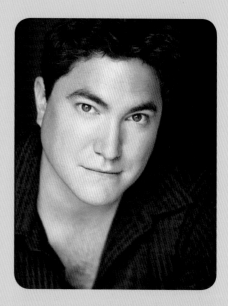

Kevin Loring is a writer and actor whose play *Where the Blood Mixes* won the prestigious Canadian Governor General's Literary Award for Drama in 2009. Kevin is a member of the Nlaka'Pamux First Nation in British Columbia and lives in Vancouver.